ALBERTO
GONZALES

ALBERTO GONZALES

ATTORNEY GENERAL

LISA TUCKER McELROY

M Millbrook Press • Minneapolis

For Zoe, my smart sweetheart of a six-year-old, who, upon hearing that I had met the biggest lawyer in the country, asked, "How tall was he?" Dream big, my big girl!

Acknowledgments: Rebecca Turner Gonzales; Maria Gonzales; Angela Williamson, Cynthia Magnuson, Tasia Scolinos, Ted Ullyot, Raquel Saus, and Courtney Elwood in the office of the attorney general; Attorney Tom Goldstein; Pam Szen (top-notch photo editor); Jean Reynolds (editor and friend extraordinaire); Darrin Schlegel, Senior Communications Specialist, Vinson & Elkins LLP; Jim Thompson, Partner, Vinson & Elkins LLP; Leah Gross, the University of Houston Law Center; Connie Barber, Librarian, MacArthur Senior High School; David Logan, Dean, Roger Williams University School of Law; Bob Ward, Dean, Southern New England School of Law; Emilie Benoit, Kim Tracey, and Amanda Browning; and Steve, Zoe, and Abby McElroy, the best family any writer could ever ask for.

Millbrook Press
A division of Lerner Publishing Group
241 First Avenue North
Minneapolis, MN 55401 U.S.A.

Website address: www.lernerbooks.com

Library of Congress Cataloging-in-Publication Data

McElroy, Lisa Tucker.
　　Alberto Gonzales : attorney general / by Lisa Tucker McElroy.
　　　　p.　　cm. — (Gateway biographies)
　　Includes bibliographical references and index.
　　ISBN-13: 978-0-8225-3418-1 (lib. bdg. : alk. paper)
　　ISBN-10: 0-8225-3418-5 (lib. bdg. : alk. paper)
　　1. Gonzales, Alberto R.　2. Attorneys general—United States—Biography.
　　I. Title.　II. Gateway biography.
　　KF373.G618M34　2006
　　340'.092—dc22　　　　　　　　　　　　　　　　　　　2005019495

Manufactured in the United States of America
1 2 3 4 5 6 – BP – 11 10 09 08 07 06

CONTENTS

Alberto R. Gonzales became the U.S. attorney general on February 3, 2005, under President George W. Bush.

He is a busy and influential man. Every day he makes very important decisions that affect the U.S. government. He often advises the president of the United States. He runs a "good team" of attorneys and other professional people across the country. He plays racquetball and golf. And, of course, he tries to get home at the end of the day to see his wife and three sons, relax a little bit, and think back on the remarkable path his life has taken.

GROWING UP IN TEXAS

Alberto R. Gonzales, attorney general of the United States, was born on August 4, 1955, in San Antonio, Texas. He was the second child and the first boy in what would eventually be a family of five boys and three girls—eight children in all.

ALBERTO'S MIDDLE INITIAL IS *R*, BUT THE INITIAL DOESN'T STAND FOR ANYTHING. HIS PARENTS GAVE HIM THE INITIAL TO HONOR HIS MOTHER, MARIA, WHOSE MAIDEN NAME WAS RODRIGUEZ.

This wedding portrait of Alberto's parents, Maria and Pablo, was taken on their wedding day in 1952.

Alberto's parents, Pablo and Maria Gonzales, were migrant workers of Mexican descent. While they were hardworking and intelligent people, they hadn't gone to school for very long. His father attended school only through the second grade. His mother only finished the sixth grade. Pablo and Maria were proud to marry in 1952. They had met in 1950 while picking cotton in the fields of western Texas.

While Maria and Pablo spoke Spanish to each other at home, they spoke only English to their children so that they would learn to speak it correctly and do well in school. As a result, the children did not learn to speak Spanish—although some of them, including Alberto, learned it later in life for professional reasons.

When Alberto was five, his parents moved from San Antonio to the North Houston neighborhood of Humble. His father and uncles built their house from scratch! The entire family of ten lived in a tiny, two-bedroom house surrounded by pine trees. It had no telephone or hot running water, but those things seemed unimportant to the Gonzales family, because they were able to rely on themselves to get what they needed. Even when times were tough, they never asked for any help from government groups.

Pablo Gonzales worked very hard at jobs as a construction worker and as a maintenance man in a rice mill so that he could support his family. Alberto recalls, "He had few opportunities because he was an uneducated man. . . . I suppose to some, he was just a common laborer. To me he was a special man who had hands that could create anything."

A CLOSE FAMILY

Alberto remembers that his family was close. His mother, a homemaker, was very supportive of her husband and children. He said, "As a young boy I begged my mother to wake me before dawn so I could share breakfast with my father before he left for work. As we ate, she would prepare a modest lunch of beans and tortillas and lovingly place them in a brown lunch sack, and we would say good-bye to him . . . the memories of

> THE ATTORNEY GENERAL LOVES MEXICAN FOOD AND ENJOYS EATING IT WHENEVER HE GETS A CHANCE. HE WOULD DROP ANYTHING, THOUGH, FOR APPLE PIE OR HIS MOM'S EMPANADAS OR HER HOMEMADE BREAD PUDDING.

this daily ritual burn strongly in my chest as I recall this simple time and simple food." Years later, when he worked in Washington, the attorney general would thank his mother by bringing her to the nation's capital to see the president in the Oval Office! Says Gonzales, "It was important to me to thank her and show her what I had accomplished because of her sacrifices. At dawn on the last day of her visit, she was up to say good-bye as I left for work, just as she had for my father on so many mornings. I think of the pride and wonder that must have filled her heart."

Maria Gonzales was a very devoted mother to her eight children—Angelica, Alberto, Antonio, Rene, Timothy, Theresa, Christina, and Paul. Maria says that Alberto and his brothers and sisters were taught to "respect their elders and their teachers, to tell the truth, and to look out for each other." She allowed them to play outside around their North Houston neighborhood. However, they had to check in with her every thirty minutes!

> MARIA GONZALES, ALBERTO'S MOTHER, STILL LIVES IN THE SMALL HOUSE IN NORTH HOUSTON WHERE ALBERTO AND HIS BROTHERS AND SISTERS GREW UP.

Maria washed all the diapers by hand and hung them out to dry on the line. At the end of each day, she would heat water on the stove so that each of the eight children could have a warm bath. She always tried to keep them healthy and safe, even when money and living space were tight.

Times were not always easy for the family. The Gonzales family was poor, but Alberto did not know that then. The children did not have many toys. Alberto remembers that on one Christmas, he received only a single toy—a G.I. Joe action figure. It was his favorite toy for quite a long time. On another Christmas, the four oldest brothers received two bicycles to share among them.

> THE ATTORNEY GENERAL'S FAVORITE HOLIDAY IS CHRISTMAS. HE LIKES HAVING HIS FAMILY AROUND HIM AND EATING LOTS OF GOOD FOOD!

Even though his family didn't have many material things, Gonzales remembers his childhood as very happy. He loved playing baseball with his four brothers and with other boys in the neighborhood. The older boys would play two-on-two all morning, until their mothers called them home for lunch. Then they would return to play outside some more until dark. Says the attorney general, "We became pretty good baseball players!" Alberto even dreamed of playing pro ball one day. Houston children were able to get free tickets to Astros games if they got straight A's in school. The attorney general remembers earning the free tickets, then walking into a pro baseball stadium for the first time thinking, "Wow!" There was only one small problem. He thought that baseball should be played outdoors. Perhaps the Astros agreed. Today, Minute Maid Park, the stadium where the Astros play, has a roof that folds back so that the players can play outdoors in good weather.

Alberto played hard, but he also worked hard. From the time he was twelve years old, he held many part-time jobs. The father of Alberto's best friend, Randy Lawson, got the two boys their first jobs selling soft drinks at football games at Rice University Stadium. Says the attorney general, "I think that Cokes cost fifty cents back then. I remember coming home from work with pockets full of quarters!" Alberto would go on to work at other jobs, like the ones he held at a local plant nursery and in retail stores. That first job at Rice really stands out in his mind, though, because it was then that it first occurred to him that he might like to attend college. At the end of the football games, he would watch the college students walking on campus and wonder what it would be like to be a Rice student. He did not know much about college, but he did know that he wanted to go to Rice and cheer for the Rice Owls.

GOING TO SCHOOL

Like family, education was very important to Pablo and Maria Gonzales. Even though Alberto's parents did not have a lot of formal education, they wanted their children to learn. Alberto and his older sister, Angie, were in the same class in school, and their parents taught them to work hard. Alberto says now, "I don't remember being afraid of many things as a child, but I do remember that I didn't want to make my parents mad!"

Alberto did well in the college preparatory classes he took at Douglas MacArthur High School in North Houston. He joined the International Club, the Christian Student Union, and the drama club. His love of sports, especially baseball, continued throughout high school. Alberto played for the MacArthur Generals on the school's varsity football and baseball teams.

Alberto *(back row, far right)* was a natural athlete. He earned a spot on his high school varsity baseball team in the early 1970s.

Alberto's adolescent years were not always easy. He has said that during his high school years he did not ask friends over to his house because he was sensitive about the fact that ten people lived in a small, cramped space. Gonzales also remembers that racial divisions were more common than they are today. While he hung out with kids of other races, most of his Hispanic class-mates did not.

Still, Alberto studied hard in high school and became a member of the National Honor Society. In 1973, when Alberto and Angie graduated from MacArthur, their parents were very proud. They were especially happy to see their children succeed and finish school because they had not had that opportunity.

JOINING THE AIR FORCE

When he graduated from high school, Gonzales was not sure what he wanted to do for a career. Although he dreamed of college, he did not think that he would be able to go. Rather, he imagined that his life would be much like his father's. He would work hard, perhaps in construction or maintenance, and support a family of his own. For a short time after he graduated, he worked as a controller at Houston's Belt and Terminal Railroad, but he soon decided to join the U.S. Air Force.

Gonzales accepted an assignment north of the Arctic Circle, in Fort Yukon, Alaska. He served there with one

Alberto marveled at the snow in Alaska, where he was stationed in 1974 while serving in the U.S. Air Force.

hundred other GIs (as servicemen and women are called) for almost twelve months–beginning in January 1974. Says Gonzales, "Even though I was used to the Texas heat, the cold didn't bother me too much."

It must have been true that the cold did not bother Gonzales too much, because some of the officers in Alaska noticed his good work. They encouraged him to apply to the U.S. Air Force Academy, a military college in Colorado Springs, Colorado. According to Gonzales, this chance to attend college seemed incredible! No one in his family had ever gone to college. First, though, he had to be accepted. He said, "Securing a nomination [or getting accepted to college] when you're at a remote

Alberto Gonzales began his college career at the U.S. Air Force Academy. He is pictured here as a sophomore.

radar site presents unique challenges. My commander made special flight arrangements for a flight surgeon to be flown up from Elmendorf Air Force Base in Anchorage for the necessary medical examination. I hopped an air force tanker plane to Fairbanks in order to take the necessary physical fitness test. I still remember doing the required pull-ups and sit-ups in an old army gym. And because I had not taken the ACT [a college entrance exam], special arrangements were made for me to take the exam alone in a small room. I had found a path to a college education, and I was prepared to do whatever was required. And, fortunately for me, I was rewarded with orders to report to the academy, and so I happily departed the frozen tundra of Alaska to pursue a new dream of being a pilot."

OFF TO COLLEGE

Alberto Gonzales was going to college! He felt very lucky, indeed. He went off to Colorado Springs with high hopes.

The Air Force Academy is part of the U.S. Air Force, so Alberto was required to learn military skills as well as academic subjects. He remembers with a smile, "I had a choice to learn to jump out of planes or fly gliders. I picked the gliders." Gonzales studied hard in the classroom, too, hoping to excel so that he could pursue a career as a pilot.

THE ATTORNEY GENERAL'S
MESSAGE TO AMERICAN CHILDREN

Alberto Gonzales realizes that he has been very lucky to have such interesting jobs. He also knows that hard work has played a large part in his success. Still, he believes that hard work is not enough. He encourages young people to find activities they love and get a good education. Then, he says, they should plan for careers that allow them to follow their passions.

Alberto Gonzales has learned this lesson well. Although he didn't enjoy college science courses as much as some of his other subjects, he didn't complain about it. Instead, he took steps to follow his dream to return to Texas and become a lawyer. His efforts to find work he loved led to his job as attorney general.

Gonzales also believes that race, gender, background, and disability should not hold children back. None of his family members ever attended college, but Alberto graduated from a top school. Although no Hispanic lawyers had previously become partners at his law firm, Gonzales was able to achieve this goal. No other Hispanic person has ever been attorney general, but that didn't stop Gonzales. He knows from personal experience that children who want to achieve can do so, no matter what they look like or where they come from.

Whatever you do, says the attorney general, do it with conviction, honor, and integrity. Be honest, and strive to be the best. Then you, too, can find a job you love and do it well.

Gonzales liked flying and being in Colorado, but he began to wonder whether he might be more interested in studying politics and law than science and engineering. He also wanted to return to Houston to be closer to his family. He decided to apply to transfer to his dream school, Rice University, the same Houston college where he had sold soft drinks many years before.

Gonzales couldn't believe it when his acceptance letter arrived from Rice. He was going home to Texas as a Rice student! He and his parents were very proud. Alberto Gonzales looked forward to learning the things he needed to know to follow the career path that he had finally chosen—that of a lawyer.

Gonzales graduated from Rice in 1979 with a degree in political science. He was the only member of his family ever to attend or graduate from college. Around that same time, Gonzales married Diane Clemens, a young woman he had met in Colorado.

Gonzales stands proudly holding his cap and gown on graduation day at Rice University in Houston, Texas.

Gonzales has a strong sense of family. Here he shares a moment with his mother at the wedding of one of his sisters in 1985.

He went on to study law in Cambridge, Massachusetts, at Harvard Law School, one of the nation's best law schools. When he graduated in 1982, he was very sad that his father could not be there. Pablo Gonzales had died just months before in an accident at work. Indeed, the attorney general has said, "If I only knew that he would die during my last semester in law school, I would have told him more often that I loved him."

BECOMING A LAWYER

Gonzales wanted to do work that would have made his father proud. That fall he began working as a business lawyer at Vinson & Elkins, a large, prestigious Houston law firm. He loved his work as a lawyer! He also enjoyed the work he began to do in the Texas Hispanic community. His law firm colleagues and friends thought he was terrific. One friend said, "Gonzales is a wonderful, caring person, an excellent lawyer with a tremendous work ethic. These are all characteristics you want in a friend, a lawyer, and a public servant." His friends in the Texas Hispanic community have often called him an important advocate for Hispanic youth.

In the late 1980s, he also impressed another man, one who would play a particularly important role in Alberto Gonzales's life (although Gonzales did not know it at the time). George H. W. Bush was, like Gonzales, a Texan, and he just happened to be the forty-first president of the United States! Bush liked Gonzales, and his staff offered him a job. Gonzales considered the offer very carefully, but he decided to try to

Gonzales and then vice president George Herbert Walker Bush were photographed together in 1986.

become a partner at his law firm instead. He was also busy teaching law at the University of Houston Law Center. He therefore declined the administration's offer, much to the surprise of many.

Gonzales's legal career was going well, but he did encounter some obstacles in his personal life. He continued to miss his father, who would have been very proud to see his son so active in the legal and Hispanic communities. His brother Rene died unexpectedly in an accident. And, in 1985, after six years of marriage, he and his wife, Diane, agreed to divorce.

Fortunately, however, in 1991, Gonzales was happy to marry a wonderful friend, Rebecca Turner, a woman whom he would later describe as "very supportive, worthy of much glory and credit." Gonzales was also grateful to become a stepfather to Rebecca's eight-year-old son, Jared Freeze.

SUCCESS ON ALL FRONTS

The next few years would be amazing and full of changes, even for someone who had accomplished as much as Alberto Gonzales! In 1991, the same year he married Rebecca, Alberto became a partner at Vinson & Elkins, the first Hispanic (along with one other new partner that year) ever to achieve that rank.

The next year, in 1992, Rebecca and Alberto welcomed a second son, Graham. Another son, Gabriel, followed soon

Alberto Gonzales and Rebecca Turner, pictured here
with Rebecca's son, Jared Freeze, were married in 1991.

after in 1995. His wife, Rebecca, was thrilled to see Gonzales take to fatherhood like a duck takes to water—he loved it! To this day, she says, the boys would rather spend time with their dad than with anyone else. "He loves them with his whole heart," she says, "and he respects them as people."

THE IMPORTANCE OF FAMILY

The birth of his children reinforced Alberto Gonzales's commitment to family. Even though he was becoming very successful as a lawyer, he still loved to spend time with his wife and sons. He often declined invitations to big parties if his family was not invited too. He recognized that the support his mother, siblings, children, and spouse gave him was critical to his success. He has said, "I . . . love my family, and they need me and I have an obligation to them. Nothing in [my] work . . . [is] as satisfying as the adoring hug of [my] child or as comforting as a warm embrace of a loyal and loving spouse. . . . All of my hopes and dreams are in my children."

As his sons grew, his career grew too. While he was so busy at work that he couldn't help his sons with their homework as often as he would have liked, he spent a lot of downtime with them over their early years. They often went to ball games and movies. He listened when they described their interests in video games and girls.

Gonzales loves spending time with his children. He is shown here with his children at a Halloween party at the Texas governor's mansion in 1996.

Although most kids have a regular bedtime, the rule became a little different in the Gonzales house: Graham and Gabriel stayed up until their dad got home so they could spend a little time together.

Gonzales and his wife loved to talk together about books they'd read and the interesting people they met. A great night out? For many years, they loved to go dancing! As their sons got older, though, dinner and movies with their children and friends and kids became regular items on the agenda.

SPORTS, FRIENDS, AND GOOD TIMES

Alberto Gonzales first began to love sports when he was a small boy in Houston. As an adult, he continued to enjoy baseball games and other professional sports events. He also loved to play sports, probably because of his competitive spirit. Once, when he worked at Vinson & Elkins, the lawyers had an obstacle course contest against law students who worked at the firm. Some of the other lawyers wanted to let the law students win. Gonzales, though, would have none of it. Even in a law firm sports competition, he was determined to win—and win he did! One friend who was also in the competition says, however, that Gonzales was a really good sport.

Gonzales also became an avid golfer. In the 1990s, he got two holes in one at a Houston golf course! He often played with his colleagues and his sons.

THE MOVE TO PUBLIC LIFE

In the early 1990s, Gonzales again learned that he had made a very positive and memorable impression on the Bush family. The newly elected Texas governor, George W. Bush, the future forty-third president of the United States, told Gonzales, "You got on my radar screen because you turned down my old man for a job."

The governor then asked Gonzales to work for him as his chief lawyer. This time, Gonzales was ready to

Gonzales continues to have opportunities to indulge his love of sports. On April 30, 2005, he was invited to throw out the opening pitch when the Washington Nationals took on the New York Mets.

make the move with his family to Austin, Texas, the state capital, and public service. Beginning in 1995 and for the next three years, he served as the governor's general counsel. His job was to advise Governor Bush on state legal matters. Gonzales did a good job, and he earned the respect of others in the state government. In fact, says his wife, Becky, Gonzales was especially good at acting as an unofficial mediator, or a calm, neutral attorney in the office. He became known as a captain in sometimes challenging seas, a cool head to whom others could turn in a crisis. Indeed, his inspirational words to Rebecca during rough times were meaningful to his colleagues too: "It'll all work out. It just has to."

From that time on, Gonzales worked in various jobs assigned to him by George W. Bush. When Bush needed a secretary of state in 1997, he appointed Fredo (as Bush likes to call him). When the Texas Supreme Court had an opening, the governor appointed his trusted adviser to be a justice. He was successful in both jobs. In the mid-to-late-1990s, Gonzales was happy in his life and career. He loved his challenging work, enjoyed living in Austin, and thrived as a husband and father. The soon-to-be president was an important influence on Gonzales. In fact,

> PRESIDENT GEORGE W. BUSH'S NICKNAME FOR ATTORNEY GENERAL GONZALES IS FREDO. THE PEOPLE IN THE ATTORNEY GENERAL'S OFFICE CALL HIM THE JUDGE, AND HIS FRIENDS CALL HIM AL. HIS FAVORITE NICKNAME? DAD.

Gonzales was sworn in as a justice of the Texas Supreme Court on January 1, 1999, by Governor George W. Bush. Gonzales's wife, Rebecca, proudly holds the Bible on which her husband is being sworn in.

the attorney general said that George W. Bush was—and is—his most important mentor and role model. "I have a great deal of respect and affection for [Bush]," he said. "When I am trying to make an important decision, I often think, what would [Bush] do?"

THE ATTORNEY GENERAL'S HIGH SCHOOL PLANTED A TREE IN HIS HONOR WHEN HE WAS A JUSTICE ON THE TEXAS SUPREME COURT.

THE MOVE TO WASHINGTON

Then his friend and mentor, George W. Bush, was elected president of the United States of America. The new president asked if Gonzales would join him in Washington. After consulting with Rebecca and their three sons, Gonzales answered, "Yes!" Hardly believing his good fortune, he began working in the West Wing of the White House. There, he advised the president of the

In December 2000, the newly elected president Bush announced his advisers. They include *(from left to right)* Alberto Gonzales, counsel to the president; Condoleezza Rice, national security adviser; and Karen Hughes, counselor to the president.

Gonzales and his two sons, Gabriel *(left)* and Graham *(right)* enjoy a tour of the Oval Office with President Bush in July 2001.

United States as counsel to the president, or the main lawyer in the White House.

In his new position, Alberto remained humble. While he was counsel to the president, he said, "As my wife Rebecca is quick to remind me, the office of the presidency did just fine before the arrival of Al Gonzales, and it will survive long after I am no longer the White House Counsel." Still, in the four years that Alberto served in the White House, he was called upon to help the president in times of crisis.

President Bush *(far right)* meets with his advisers *(from left to right)* Alberto Gonzales, Karen Hughes, Condoleezza Rice, Ari Fleischer, and Andrew Card after the terrorist attacks on September 11, 2001.

He greeted the president on the South Lawn of the White House on September 11, 2001, and he helped provide advice to the president that day and in the weeks that followed, talking with him on how to respond to the terrorist attacks. He advised the president when the United States went to war in Afghanistan and Iraq. He supported President Bush when the chief executive had to make decisions on national and foreign policy. Said Gonzales at the time, "I cannot imagine a better job as a lawyer, and I cannot think of a more inspirational place to work."

BECOMING ATTORNEY GENERAL

Perhaps there was at least one even more interesting job. John Ashcroft, the attorney general of the United States, decided to step down after George W. Bush was reelected in 2004. The second-term president asked Alberto Gonzales to fill the job. Before he could take the job, however, Gonzales's nomination would have to be approved by the Senate.

Gonzales's Senate confirmation hearings were somewhat difficult. Many senators thought that Gonzales would be a great attorney general, but some others disagreed. His

On November 10, 2004, President Bush announced that Gonzales was his nominee to replace former attorney general John Ashcroft.

Photographers snapped pictures of Gonzales as he arrived at his confirmation hearings before the Senate Judiciary Committee on January 6, 2005.

supporters had to explain to the other senators what a great person and lawyer Alberto Gonzales was. A senator from Pennsylvania said, "I have always found him [Alberto Gonzales] to be completely forthright, brutally honest—in some cases telling me things I did not want to hear but always forthright, always honest, sincere, serious. This is a serious man who takes the responsibilities that have been given to him as a great privilege and a great honor which he holds very carefully and gently in his hands." Said another senator, this one from Kentucky, "Judge Gonzales is proof that in America, there are no artificial barriers to success. A man or a woman can climb to any height that his or her talents can take them. For Judge Gonzales, that is a very high altitude indeed. And luckily for his country, he is not quite finished climbing yet."

The other senators listened carefully. In the end, the news was good. On February 3, 2005, Gonzales was confirmed as attorney general by a Senate vote of 60–36. On that day, at his official swearing in, he took the oath of office, administered by Vice President Richard Cheney, on a Bible belonging to his son Graham. His wife, sons, and mother proudly attended his ceremonial swearing in two weeks later. Associate Justice of the Supreme Court Sandra Day O'Connor administered the oath of office,

Gonzales's family and President Bush look on as he is sworn into office as U.S. attorney general by Associate Justice of the Supreme Court Sandra Day O'Connor in February 2005.

Photographed proudly with his family and President Bush, Attorney General Alberto Gonzales stands ready to take on the demands of his new job.

and this time, the new attorney general swore his oath on a Bible that belonged to his youngest son, Gabriel.

THE ATTORNEY GENERAL'S JOB

The attorney general's website states that Alberto Gonzales is "the head of the Department of Justice and chief law enforcement officer of the federal government." He oversees the U.S. attorneys, the top federal

> ALBERTO GONZALES IS THE FIRST HISPANIC ATTORNEY GENERAL AND THE HIGHEST-RANKING HISPANIC GOVERNMENT OFFICIAL EVER.

lawyers in each state. He gives legal advice to the president and the president's employees in the executive branch of the U.S. government. He may argue cases for the U.S. government before the Supreme Court. He is in charge of hundreds of lawyers across the country that work hard to make sure that the United States is a safe and lawful place to live.

His job is a very difficult one, and he works very long hours. He jokes that he would like to go to bed early, but he rarely gets the chance. Most evenings, he especially misses being home for dinner with his wife and young sons.

Alberto Gonzales says that his work in the U.S. government has been very demanding but very fulfilling. As attorney general, he must help solve very large problems. "The President charges his Cabinet to play big ball," he says. Gonzales notes that the issues he deals with have major consequences and that he is always in the public eye. "I can't fret," he emphasizes. "I have to surround myself with good people and build a good team." He knows that others may view some decisions he makes to be mistakes. He points out, "This is hard stuff that we deal with in Washington." However, every single day, he must trust himself, his judgment, and his honor to do what's right for the United States.

> ALBERTO GONZALES IS SEVENTH IN LINE TO SUCCEED TO THE U.S. PRESIDENCY.

Alberto Gonzales says that his favorite part of being AG is making a difference. "I enjoy using the majestic power of the Justice Department to help Americans," he says. The hardest part? Looking at the tough legal questions that come his way. Although it's hard work to figure out the answers, he enjoys the challenge and the privilege of looking at important issues. He knows that these issues affect thousands, even millions of

On September 8, 2005, Gonzales strategized with Vice President Dick Cheney *(left)* and Homeland Security Secretary Michael Chertoff *(right)* during a trip to Baton Rouge, Louisiana, in the weeks following Hurricane Katrina, which wreaked havoc on the Gulf Coast of the United States.

Americans, and he tries hard to find solutions to the problems that they face.

Some of these difficult legal issues have to do with families and children. As a dad, Gonzales knows how hard it is to raise children. As a lawyer, he wants to do everything he can to help parents protect their kids. Through his job as AG, he can work on passing laws that help find missing children, get rid of illegal drugs, and shield kids from harmful material on the Internet.

Alberto Gonzales loves his job. He marvels that the son of a cotton picker and a construction worker could hold the top legal job in the country.

THE ATTORNEY GENERAL'S DAY

A typical day in the AG's office is very long and busy. Gonzales arrives at his office very early, often before the sun is up. He spends an hour reading and looking at his calendar, then meets with his staff and other government officials until mid-morning. He misses seeing the president every day (as he did when he worked in the White House), but in this early morning time, he often talks with the president. Often there will be a conversation with the head of the FBI, as well as Justice Department lawyers.

THE ATTORNEY GENERAL LOVES THE COLOR RED. HE SOMETIMES WEARS BRIGHT RED TIES TO WORK AT HIS OFFICE IN THE DEPARTMENT OF JUSTICE.

Later in the day, he often travels (such as when he visited Louisiana to help victims of Hurricane Katrina), gives speeches, and visits the White House. His meetings last until well into the evening!

Then there are the special days. One Fourth of July, for example, the attorney general visited U.S. troops in Iraq. He remembers flying into Iraq one weekend all the way from the United States, then almost having to turn back because of a sandstorm. The helicopter almost couldn't land because of all the sand! Just when he thought that he'd never be able to leave the airport, an army general got some helicopters to come in like the

The Attorney General spoke to U.S. troops during a surprise visit to Iraq on July 3, 2005.

cavalry and take him to the embassy. There, he had the
chance to meet the president of Iraq and the Department
of Justice staffers who were in Iraq helping write a new
constitution and set up the court system. Perhaps the
most amazing part of his trip to Iraq? He did it all in
one weekend! He did not even stop to sleep until he was
on the plane home.

DREAMS DO COME TRUE

One thing is certain—Alberto Gonzales is very glad that
he left private law practice to go into public service.
Although when he moved to Austin and then to
Washington, D.C., he made less money, he and his wife
have no doubt that the sacrifice was definitely worth it.
In public service positions, he can help many more people than he could in private practice. What's more, he
strongly believes that his beginnings as a young lawyer
at a Houston law firm gave him the confidence and
skills he needs to serve his country. He says, "Each experience more than satisfies the hopes and dreams I had as
a young man to do something with my life that would
make a difference."

What's next for Alberto Gonzales? Many people
believe that he could be an important political figure in his
own right. What does Gonzales think? "It will take care of
itself," he says. "As long as I feel passion and commitment
for what I do, everything will work out just fine."

MORE FUN FACTS ABOUT
ALBERTO GONZALES

- The AG rides his bike up to twenty-two miles each day! He's so fast that his wife and sons can't even keep up.

- The AG has two pets. His dog, Sasha, an American Eskimo/Shetland sheepdog mix, was rescued from an Austin animal shelter. He also has a parakeet named Turquoise. Guess what color his feathers are?

- Alberto Gonzales's favorite movies are the *Star Wars* series. He really liked seeing the last movie with his sons, but they didn't dress up in costumes to attend the show!! Before he married Becky, he had a whole room in his house filled with *Star Wars* souvenirs.

- Alberto Gonzales likes Shakespeare's plays a lot, especially *Romeo and Juliet.*

- The AG often eats breakfast for dinner! He likes bacon, tortillas, and eggs over medium.

- The Attorney General was thrilled in 2005 when his favorite team, the Houston Astros, made it to the World Series for the first time.

CHRONOLOGY

August 4, 1955	Alberto R. Gonzales is born in San Antonio, Texas.
1973	Graduates from Douglas MacArthur Senior High School with high honors
1974–1975	Serves in the U.S. Air Force in Fort Yukon, Alaska
1975–1977	Attends the U.S. Air Force Academy
1977	Transfers to Rice University
1979	Graduates from Rice University with a degree in political science
1982	Graduates from Harvard Law School
Late 1980s	Meets and impresses George H. W. Bush
1991	Marries Rebecca (Becky) Turner Becomes a partner at Vinson & Elkins, LLP
1992	Son, Alberto Graham Gonzales, is born

1995	Appointed general counsel to Texas governor George W. Bush
	Son, Gabriel Quinn Gonzales, is born
1997	Appointed Texas secretary of state by Texas governor George W. Bush
1999	Appointed by Texas governor George W. Bush to be a justice on the Texas Supreme Court
2000	Runs for and wins election to keep Texas Supreme Court seat
2001	Appointed counsel to the president by President George W. Bush
2005	Appointed U.S. attorney general by President George W. Bush

GLOSSARY

attorney general: the head of the Department of Justice. His or her job is to advise the president of the United States and to oversee all U.S. attorneys.

counsel to the president: the president's chief lawyer. He or she gives legal advice to the president about White House matters.

Department of Justice: the government office where the attorney general works. Its job is to enforce our nation's laws and help prevent crime. It is sometimes called the "DOJ."

law firm: a group of lawyers who work together, usually in private practice

legal issue: a question about something pertaining to the law

mediator: a neutral person who helps others solve their legal problems without going to court

private practice: a private organization, such as a law firm

public service: to work for the state or federal government; to serve the people

senate confirmation hearings: open discussions in the U.S. Senate about a candidate's qualifications for a job such as attorney general. At the end of the hearings, the senators vote to confirm or reject the candidate for the job.

Supreme Court justice: a judge on the Supreme Court or on the highest state court

U.S. attorney: a lawyer who works for and defends the United States

FURTHER READING

There are no other books for young readers about Alberto Gonzales. However, these websites have information about him:

"Attorney General Alberto R. Gonzales Biography" *United States Department of Justice*
http://www.usdoj.gov/ag/aggonzalesbio.html

"Biography: Alberto R. Gonzales" *Academy of Achievement*
http://www.achievement.org/autodoc/page/gon0bio-1

INDEX

Page numbers in *italics* refer to illustrations.

SOURCE NOTES

Unless otherwise noted, all direct quotes in this manuscript came from a series of interviews between the author, Alberto Gonzales, Rebecca Turner Gonzales, and Maria Gonzales:

Interviews with Alberto Gonzales: May 31, 2005, and October 4, 2005

Interviews with Rebecca Turner Gonzales: August 19, 2005, and multiple dates thereafter

Interview with Maria Gonzales: August 19, 2005

9 Alberto Gonzales (Commencement speech, Rice University Houston, May 2004).

9–10 Ibid.

10 Lois Romano, "Positioned for a Call to Justice," *Washington Post*, July 10, 2001, C01.

17 Alberto Gonzales, speech.

20 Ibid.

21 Author interview with Jim Thompson, Vinson & Elkins partner, June 21, 2005.

24 Alberto Gonzales, speech.

26 Chitra Ragavan, "Bush's Legal Eagle, Rising with the Son," *U.S. News & World Report,* March 12, 2001 http://www.usnews.com/usnews/news/articles/010312/archive_003347.htm (October 21, 2005).

31 Alberto Gonzales, speech.

32 Ibid.

34 Senator Rick Santorum, Executive Session, Nomination of Alberto R. Gonzales to be Attorney General of the United States, S923-02, 109th Cong., 1st sess., *Congressional Record* 151 (February 3, 2005).

34–35 Senator Mitch McConnell, Executive Session, Nomination of Alberto R. Gonzales to be Attorney General of the United States, S923-02, 109th Cong., 1st sess., *Congressional Record* 151 (February 3, 2005).

36 "Office of the Attorney General," *United States Department of Justice,* n.d., http://www.usdoj.gov/ag/ (October 20, 2005).

41 Alberto Gonzales, speech.

PHOTO ACKNOWLEDGMENTS